Un

Live and Learn

Mc
Graw
Hill
Education

Contents

Ray Saves the Play

Ray took a break from his jobs
at home and rode straight over to
April's. April and five pals were about
to unveil a new play. Ray was thrilled.
Ray often hoped that he could get a
good part in a nice play.

"Hey, April," said Ray. "May I take a part? I could be a neighing horse or a white cat with stripes."

"All the acting parts are taken," April said. "But you can help. Get that big tree. It has a place on stage."

3

Just then, April's dog, Max, sprang up and hit the tree. It split in two. Paint splashed and sprayed on the grass and shrubs. Max made a mess!

"The tree is crushed!" said April. "There's paint on it, too."

"Wait a second. I've got a great idea," said Ray. "I have to get strong white fabric."

"What about a big white sheet?" said April's dad. "I've got one. I'll get it. You can use it in the play."

While April's dad rushed to get a sheet, Ray got Max.

Ray said to Max, "Let's get some thin branches. Do not scrape or scratch me with them, Max. We'll play fetch with them in just a bit."

April's dad got the sheet. It looked like a long white veil. It was just the right size. Ray cut holes in it.

April smiled at Ray. "This is such a good plan! Now you can be in the play!" said April. "It will be fun!"

Around eight, the six kids got
on stage. They took their places in
a line. Ray thrust his arms open as
wide as the world. Then he raised
his branches up. His pals yelled and
clapped. Ray was a hit in the play.

The Great Plains

The Great Plains is a nice place with big wide open spaces. It is inside of the United States.

On the Great Plains on a day with sun, what main things can you see? Big hay bales sit, fat, in the sun's hot rays. Swaying waves of grain move with grace in wind on the Great Plains.

Philip Coblentz/AGE Fotostock

A lot of nice long grass waves against a wide sky. At daybreak, if it is not hot, hike on a trail in the Great Plains. But stop! Wait! Take a break. Two fox pups are playing in the long waving hay.

The Great Plains has sun, but it can rain. The sky can be gray. Try and stay dry! You may see a great big rainbow.

Eight Is Great!

Let's say it's your eighth birthday.
Try eight nice things on this day.

13

If it is a day with sun, sit in the sun's rays. They're nice and hot.

Take a hike to a lake. Eight is a great age.

14

Christopher Futcher/iStock/Getty Images Plus/
Getty Images

If it is not hot, you can ice skate.
You can play when it is not hot.

Play in snow and make fun shapes.
Eight is a great age.

If it is hot, go to a nice sand beach and wade in salt water.

Wade in up to your waist. Play in fun waves! Eight is such a great age!

If it's raining, just stay inside and play two fun games.

Make nice shapes with play clay, and then paint them. Eight is such a great age!

Whether it is hot or not, bake a great cake! It's a good thing to make. Hey, Eight is such a great age!

What a Day!

An ape ate seven grapes in space.
What did he say? "They're great!"

Two snails, Gail and Dale, had a play date. They planned to sail, but mom said that it may rain. What did they say? "Okay. Let's play games."

A gray whale named Jay swam in a
lake. He weighed a lot. His tail was red
and pink. And the whale, Jay, rode the
white splashing waves.

Then my dad said my name. "Hey,
May! Wake up. Did you have a nice
dream? It is like a play that takes
place inside of your brain!"

High
in the Sky

At night, take a break. Lie in the grass and gaze up high in the sky. You might find a hundred silent stars right over your home. A bunch of bright dots shining in a night sky is quite a sight! Try taking a look up!

Why do stars shine in the sky?

Stars shine because they are made up of hot gases that let off light. They can look either bright or faint. They may be red, blue, white, or yellow. Stars are great!

The Earth   White Dwarf   Neutron Star

Are stars the same size?

Stars are not the same size. Lots are as big as the sun! And the sun is big! They are huge, but they may look like dots. That is because those stars are in places far off in space!

Which star is closest?

The sun is closest. It is hot and bright. It lights the day time. At night, it sets. Without the sun, the earth would be cold.

What shapes do stars make?

Stars spaced apart in the sky can look like basic shapes. You may not find an apron or dad's tie, but you can find a big dog. You can also find a lion and a big whale with a tail.

28

Illustration: Roger Radtke

More than eight bright stars make this shape. It is not a freight train or a bride with a veil. It is not a kite on a string or a fat cat with a hat. What shape is it? Why, it is a ram. Can you find its thin legs?

29

How can you spy on stars?

To spy at the sky, you can use a big telescope like this. The lens makes things big. It is fun to watch the night sky. Begin watching stars. You'll see why it is fun!

Steve Cole/Photodisc/Getty Images

A Bright Flight

Hi. My name is Sy and I like flying places. My last flight was on July Fourth!

"Have a nice flight," the pilot said.
"It's a fine day to fly." Then, we went up
high in the big, wide sky. When it was
dining time, I ate rice and a slice of pie.

32

By night, we had almost arrived.
A man said, "Right outside is quite a
sight!" A man by a window was kind
and did not mind if I leaned over.

I just saw a slight light. But then I saw those bright fireworks from way up high! A wild sight!

"My, my! It was wise to fly tonight! Such a bright flight!" my mom said and smiled.

Three Goats
—and—
a Troll

Three goats looked up at a huge hill as high as the sky.

"Goats must munch on grass to stay fit," said Joe Goat.

"Let's go over Troll's low bridge to find grass on the hill," said Moe Goat.

Doe Goat started to go over.

"Who is that?" croaked Troll. "I like goats. I will eat you up bite by bite!"

"But I am only as big as your toe!" yelled Doe. "Wait for Moe. Moe is better. You will get more to eat," said Doe.

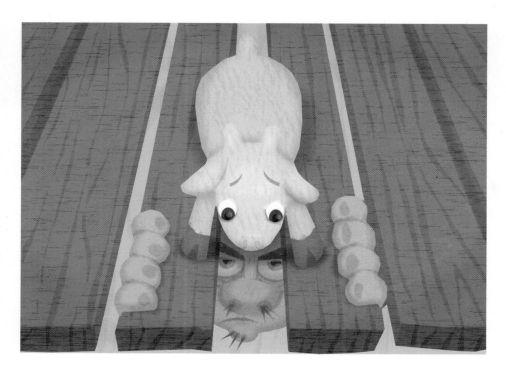

Moe Goat started to go over.

"That must be Moe," said Troll. "He will be my lunch! I can't wait!"

"Hold on!" said Moe. "Wait for Joe if you don't mind. He's the best of our group. And that is not a lie."

Joe Goat started to go over.

"You must be Joe," said Troll.
"I will throw you on a big plate. You
will be better than a fresh pie," Then
Troll stepped up on the low bridge.

"No, you won't!" yelled Joe.
"I will throw you right in this lake!"
And that's just what Joe did.

"My coat is soaked!" moaned Troll.

"So long!" yelled Doe, Moe, and
Joe. And they ran to munch on grass.

A Rose Grows

Westend61/Getty Images

In a big city, growing a rose garden is nice. A lot of people can help make it grow well.

A Big Goal

Kids go to help a rose garden grow. This is a big goal. They hope to make the city a nice place. And roses will be a nice and safe home for birds.

Ariel Skelley/Blend Images/Getty Images

Go and Grow!

A group shows things to the kids, like coaches. They use a hoe. They are pros and can help a lot. They can make those roses grow, grow, grow.

Growing Rows

Yellow roses grow in a row. Red Roses grow in a row. Pink roses grow in a row. They're slow to grow, but they're so nice.

Grow, roses! Grow, grow, grow.

Sneaky Mouse had a secret meeting. She was tired of fleeing from Beast. Beast was a mean cat!

So Sneaky got a few old pals. He and Joe, Moe, Pete, and Stanley met for tea and a big piece of cheese.

46

"What can we do about Beast before we get hurt?" asked Sneaky. "Let's hear from Pete first."

"Every day we can go hide in that big field we mow. Beast will not see us. We'll be safe," said Pete.

"I have a special plan!" said
Sneaky. "Let me show you this big
bell. It is key to my plan. We will tie
this bell on Beast. Then we will hear
Beast before she can feast on us!"

After that, every mouse was happy but Stanley. He sat still with his feet up.

"Will it be easy?" asked Stanley. "Tell me how we will get a bell on Beast. He is fast. And he is mean!"

49

Each mouse sat still. Then they spotted Beast. Pete moaned. Joe groaned. Stanley was right. It seemed that this plan would not be so easy after all. These mice would need a much better plan!

The Beach Is a Treat

It's the weekend! You are lucky if you can go to the beach and sit by the sea.

Have a seat on a towel or sheet. Read a story here. Feel the breeze. What might you see at the beach? See heaps of sand and many tiny shells. Look for happy families and sandy babies! Maybe you will even see a few seals swimming free in the deep sea! Would you like to be a seal?

If the heat bothers you, go feel the waves on your feet. But stay safe at the beach. Do not go in deep water, and put on sunscreen. Try not to get sand in your eyes. That is key. The sand can really hurt!

Liv Friis-Larsen/iStock/Getty Images Plus/Getty Images

If you are hungry, you can eat a beach treat like a peach or sweet berries. If your hands get sticky, put them in the sea to keep them clean. Then, fall asleep in the breeze!

Luke had come from India to live in America with his dad, Steve.

"This field needs green plants," Luke told Dad. "I will grow a few plants. In a brief time, they'll grow to be nice and big. Just wait and see!"

Luke saw a sunny spot and dug holes. He began planting seeds. He used a watering can to give them a drink.

Luke watched these seeds every day. But he didn't see a green leaf.

"Why won't my plants grow?" asked
Luke. "In my country, plants grow
big and beautiful. What can I do?"

Luke turned and climbed up on
a huge stone. He gazed at the blue
sky and dreamed about home.

"It is not fun to plant new seeds that do not grow," said Luke.

Luke began making music. He hummed a sweet tune that made him think of home. He liked to hum while he was making a plan.

The next day was the greatest!
His plants had grown. It was true!
Luke was happy. Music was the key.

Luke hummed to his plants every
day. Dad played music on his flute.
The plants grew and grew!

Mules

"As stubborn as a mule" means to argue and refuse to change your mind. But mules aren't really that stubborn!

donkey

horse

mule

A mule's dad is a donkey and its mom is a horse. Mules are huge. They can weigh as much as 1,000 pounds! And mules are strong. They are used for carrying heavy loads. A mule can climb steep hills, too.

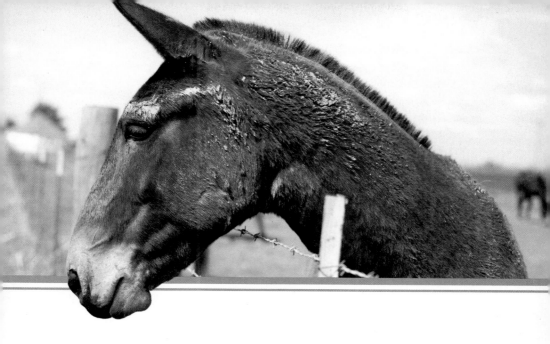

Mule hair is in hues of black, gray, brown, or white. Mules have long ears, short manes, and thick necks. They have strong teeth and they eat less than horses eat. To live, mules eat grain, hay, and grasses. But they can be picky eaters!

This mule is so beautiful and cute. It is not huge yet. Its dad is a donkey. Its mom is a horse. It's a mule!

Growing Stew

On those days when spring began,
we tilled the garden and planted new
seeds. What plants will those new
seeds be? What will the garden
give us?

The birds and bugs made music as
we kept the garden clean. The wind
blew chilly, as spring was new, but
a few buds came breaking through.
Which new plants are growing?

The truth is, it's not easy to help those new buds grow, but this garden was a duty. So we kept feeding the new baby plants.

In the garden, the plants are veggies. They grew in rain and wind and dew. We pulled the weeds and fed the plants. We chased off the harmful birds and bugs, like ants.

The veggies grew in June and July.
Then, we picked them. We pulled up
beautiful carrots, peas and beans. We
put them in a big pot. Yum! It was a lot
of time but we ate a tasty stew. What
a special menu!

Dan and Jen Made Music

Dan and Jen both liked music. They played music each day. For Dan and Jen, any time was a great time to make music.

Dan liked to play the flute. He blew a few tunes on his flute. His music was high and sweet. But Jen did not like it. Jen did not want to be mean, but she went away when Dan began.

72

Jen liked to play the drum. Jen
made a big bang on a drum. Jen's
music was very low and deep. Dan did
not like the sound of it. He went away,
too. And Jen knew why.

Then, Dan and Jen played together.
They made new music that is low and
deep and high and sweet. They both
think it is great. They made beautiful
new music. What a way to live!

DECODABLE WORDS
Target Phonics Elements
Long a: *a** April; ***ai*:*** paint, raised, straight, wait; ***ay*:*** may, play, Ray, sprayed; ***ea*:** break, great; ***ei*:** unveil, veil; ***ey*:** hey, they

HIGH-FREQUENCY WORDS
about, around, good, great, idea, part, second, two, world
Review: could, do, from, he, looked, me, new, now, open, or, over, right, said, some, the, their, to, too, took, was, were, you
Story Words: arms, be, horse, tree, sheet

The Great Plains

DECODABLE WORDS
Target Phonics Elements
Long a: *ai*:* grain, main, plains, rain, trail, wait; ***ay*:*** day, daybreak, gray, hay, may, rays, stay, swaying; ***ea*:** break, daybreak, great

HIGH-FREQUENCY WORDS
two
Review: see, the, to, what, with, you
Story Words: dry, sky

Eight Is Great!

DECODABLE WORDS
Target Phonics Elements
Long a: *a*:* game, lake, shapes, skate, wade, waves; ***ai*:*** paint, raining, waist; ***ay*:*** clay, play, rays, say, stay; ***ea*:** great; ***eigh:*** eight, eighth; ***ey*:*** hey, they

HIGH-FREQUENCY WORDS
good, two
Review: go, not, make, play, the, to, up, you, your, water
Story Words: beach, snow, sun, whether

What a Day!

DECODABLE WORDS
Target Phonics Elements
Long a: *ai*:* brain, sails, snails, rain, tail; ***ay*:*** day, gray, Jay, may, play, say; ***ea*:*** great; ***eigh:*** weighed; ***ey*:*** hey, they

HIGH-FREQUENCY WORDS
two
Review: my, said, the, they, to, two, was, what, you, your
Story Words: dream, swam

Previously Taught

High in the Sky

DECODABLE WORDS
Target Phonics Elements
  Long *i*: *i**: find, lion, silent; *y**: sky, spy, try, why; *igh**: light, might, night, right, sight; *ie**: lie, tie

HIGH-FREQUENCY WORDS
also, apart, begin, either, hundred, over, places, those, which, without
Review: are, because, blue, do, how, look, of, or, see, the, to, what, yellow, you, your
Story Words: closest, live, star, stars, telescope

A Bright Flight

WORD COUNT: 122

DECODABLE WORDS
Target Phonics Elements
  Long *i*: *i**: hi, kind, mind, pilot, wild; *y**: by, fly, my, sky; *igh**: bright, high, flight, light, night, right, sight, slight; *ie**: pie

HIGH-FREQUENCY WORDS
those, places
Review: almost, from, have, over, said, saw, the, to, was, we, went
Story Words: arrived, fireworks, fourth, leaned, outside, window

---

Three Goats and a Troll

DECODABLE WORDS
Target Phonics Elements
  Long *o*: *o**: go, no, so, Troll; *oa**: coat, croaked, goat, goats, moaned, soaked; *ow**: throw; *oe**: Doe, Joe, Moe, toe

HIGH-FREQUENCY WORDS
better, group, long, more, only, our, started, three, who
Review: for, he, looked, of, over, the, to, what, you
Story Words: be, eat

A Rose Grows

WORD COUNT: 122

DECODABLE WORDS
Target Phonics Elements
  Long *o*: *o**: go, home, pros, rose, so; *oa**: coaches, goal; *ow**: grow, growing, grows, row, rows, shows, slow, yellow; *oe**: hoe

HIGH-FREQUENCY WORDS
group
Review: are, they, to, use
Story Words: city, garden

Previously Taught

It Won't Be Easy   WORD COUNT: 197

DECODABLE WORDS
Target Phonics Elements
   Long e: e*: be, he, secret, she, we; **ee***:
cheese, feet, fleeing, meeting, need, see,
seemed; **ea***: Beast, each, easy, mean,
tea; **ie***: field, piece; **y:** happy, Sneaky;
ey*: key, Stanley;
e_e*: Pete, these

HIGH-FREQUENCY WORDS
after, before, every, few, first,
hear, hurt, old, special, would
Review: about, all, better, do,
for, from, have, how, of, said, to,
was, what, you
Story Words: mouse

The Beach Is a Treat   WORD COUNT: 155

DECODABLE WORDS
Target Phonics Elements
   Long e: e*: be, even, maybe; **ee***: asleep,
breeze, deep, feel, feet, free, keep, see,
sheet, sunscreen, sweet, weekend; **ea***:
beach, clean, eat, heat, heaps, peach,
read, sea, seal, seat, treat; **ie**: babies; **y***:
happy, hungry, lucky, many, sandy, sticky,
tiny

HIGH-FREQUENCY WORDS
few, would, hurt
Review: are, do, fall, have, here,
of, or, them, to, what, you, your,
water
Story Words: bothers, towel

Luke's Tune   WORD COUNT: 136

DECODABLE WORDS
Target Phonics Elements
   Long u: u_e*: flute, tune; **ew***: few,
blew, new; **u***: music

HIGH-FREQUENCY WORDS
America, beautiful, began,
climbed, come, country, didn't,
give, live, turned
Review: about, do, every, for,
from, of, said, saw, to, was,
what
Story Words: India

Mules   WORD COUNT: 141

DECODABLE WORDS
Target Phonics Elements
   Long u: u_e*: cute, huge, mule,
refuse, used; **ue***: argue

HIGH-FREQUENCY WORDS
beautiful, live
Review: are, change, of, have,
than, that, they, to, your
Story Words: donkey, horse,
long, short, stubborn

Previously Taught   **77**

Growing Stew
WORD COUNT: 163

DECODABLE WORDS
Target Phonics Elements
  Long *u*: *ew**: stew, new, grew; *u**:
  music, truth, duty, menu

HIGH-FREQUENCY WORDS
  began, beautiful, give
  Review: special, what

Dan and Jen Made Music
WORD COUNT: 136

DECODABLE WORDS
Target Phonics Elements
  Long *u, u*:* flute, music

HIGH-FREQUENCY WORDS
  beautiful, began, live
  Review: are, at, very
  Story Word: beautiful

Previously Taught

HIGH FREQUENCY WORDS

Grade K

a	around	green	question	almost	great	says
and	away	grow	right	also	green	school
are	be	guess	round	America	group	second
can	been	happy	run	and	grow	see
come	before	hard	school	another	has	seven
do	began	heard	should	any	have	she
does	better	help	small	apart	he	should
for	blue	her	so	are	hear	show
go	boy	how	some	around	help	sky
good	brother	instead	soon	baby	here	small
has	brought	into	start	ball	how	some
have	build	jump	sure	beautiful	hundred	sounds
he	busy	knew	surprise	because	hurt	special
help	buy	know	their	before	idea	start
here	by	large	then	began	into	started
I	call	laugh	there	begin	isn't	straight
is	carry	learn	they	better	know	the
like	caught	listen	thought	bird	learn	their
little	children	live	three	blue	leaves	there
look	climb	love	through	both	light	they
me	color	make	today	boy	like	this
my	come	many	together	buy	little	those
of	could	money	tomorrow	by	live	three
play	day	month	too	change	long	to
said	does	more	toward	cheer	look	too
see	done	mother	two	climbed	me	took
she	door	move	under	cold	more	try
the	down	near	up	come	move	turned
they	early	new	upon	could	my	two
this	eat	no	very	country	new	under
to	eight	none	use	didn't	now	understands
too	enough	not	walk	do	number	until
want	every	nothing	want	done	of	walk
was	eyes	now	warm	early	off	want
we	fall	of	water	eight	often	was
what	father	oh	way	either	old	wash
where	favorite	old	were	even	on	water
who	few	once	what	every	one	were
with	find	one	who	fall	only	what
you	flew	only	why	family	open	where
	food	or	woman	far	or	which
	found	other	wonder	few	orange	who
Grade 1	four	our	work	field	other	why
about	friend	out	would	find	our	without
above	from	over	write	first	out	won
after	front	people	year	five	over	won't
again	full	picture	young	flower	part	work
ago	fun	place	your	food	picture	world
all	girl	poor		for	places	would
animal	give	pretty	**Grade 2**	friends	play	year
another	gone	pull	about	funny	pull	yellow
answer	good	push	after	girl	put	yes
any	great	put	all	give	ready	you
				go	right	your
				goes	said	
				good	saw	

DECODING SKILLS TAUGHT TO DATE

short *a, i; -s, -es* (plural nouns); short *e, o, u; -s, -es* (inflectional endings); two-letter blends: *r*-blends, *s*-blends, *t*-blends, *l*-blends; closed syllables; short *a*, long *a: a_e; -ed, -ing* (inflectional endings); short *i*, long *i: i_e;* possessives; short *o*, long *o: o_e;* short *u*, long *u: u_e; -ed, -ing* (w/doubling final consonants; drop final *e*); CVC*e* syllables; soft *c* and *g: dge, ge, lge, nge, rge;* prefixes *re-, un-, dis-;* consonant digraphs *ch, -tch, sh, ph, th, ng, wh;* suffixes *-ful, -less;* three-letter blends: *scr, spr, str, thr, spl, shr;* compound words; long *a: a, ai, ay, ea, ei, eigh, ey;* contractions with *'s, 're, 'll, 've;* long *i: i, y, igh, ie;* open syllables; long *o: o, oa, ow, oe;* contractions with *not;* long *e: e, ee, ea, ie, y, ey, e_e; -s, -es* (change *y* to *i*); long *u: u_e, ew, ue, u;* comparative endings *-er, -est*